City Garden

by Albert Ruiz
illustrated by John Nez

Table of Contents

D1418169

The World Outside

Matt looked out of his new home.

He looked at the empty lot
across the street.

Trash was on the ground.

Mrs. Choi sat with her dog, Pepper. She waved to Matt.

Matt liked Mrs. Choi and Pepper. He enjoyed their company.

Matt and Mrs. Choi Help

Matt came outside. He saw a crack in the lot. A tiny flower was growing there.

Matt was delighted to see the flower.

"I think there is a garden under here," Matt said.

Mrs. Choi smiled. "I think so, too," she said.

They made a plan.

The next day Matt and
Mrs. Choi made a poster.
Then they put it up.

The poster said: *Please sign our letter to the mayor. We want to make the lot into a wonderful garden.*

Hard Work Pays Off

A letter from the mayor came!
They could plant a garden.

People had many ideas
to share about the garden.

Matt's dad brought a big machine. It cleaned out the lot.

People were working in the garden every weekend.

Matt was thinning out the thick weeds.

Summer came. Plants filled the garden.

Matt and Mrs. Choi made a big pot of soup.

Everyone picked flowers and ate soup. They enjoyed the garden party!

Comprehension Check

Retell the Story

Use a Plot Chart and the pictures to help you retell this story.

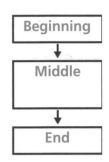

Think and Compare

1. Turn to pages 6–7. Why did Matt think there was a secret garden under the concrete? *(Analyze Plot)*

2. What would you like to fix in your neighborhood? How could your neighbors help you? *(Apply)*

3. Why is it good to take care of the land around your home? *(Evaluate)*